the Backroom

[A PLAY]

i

THIRD EDITION

HOPE MAXWELL-SNYDER

ii

THIRD EDITION

Somondoco Press

Designed by Perk Hull

Acknowledgments

My heartfelt thanks to Jiri Zizka for his thoughtful feedback, Perk Hull for his outstanding cover and design, Ed Herendeen and Carl Tribble Jr. for their valuable suggestions. William, Stephany, Sara, Mike and John, you are always listening. Special thanks to Bill Schley for his technical expertise and passionate involvement in all my work.

For Mike and John, where would the Mongolian
Princess be without her bodyguards?

Contents

Act 1

Act 2

Cast of Characters

MONICA DELGADO   AGE 42, PRESIDENTIAL CANDIDATE

HELENA MAYO   AGE 38, TELEVISION REPORTER. USED TO BE A NEWSPAPER REPORTER

JUAN
MALE GUARD   AGE 16, IN CHARGE OF MONICA AND HELENA

ASUNCION
FEMALE GUARD   AGE 30, SOMETIMES IN CHARGE OF MONICA AND HELENA

COMANDANTE AGUJA   AGE 45, GUERRILLA LEADER (REAL NAME IS ARMANDO)

Setting

The time is the present.
The place a country somewhere in Latin America
during the struggle between the government
and the guerrilla fighters.

A guerrilla camp.
Three days before Christmas eve.

Faith is the strength by which a shattered world shall emerge into the light.

Helen Keller

the Backroom

Act 1

Scene One

Midnight. A dark stark room with two cots, a table and two chairs. MONICA and HELENA are asleep on the cots. MONICA is sensual and curvaceous; she has dark hair. HELENA'S hair is dyed blond. She's thin. Both women wear military uniforms. While the room is dark we hear helicopters and shooting, followed by a Gregorian chant and then "Our Father" recited in Spanish and English by MONICA, HELENA, ASUNCION, JUAN and COMANDANTE AGUJA, first separately and then together. The prayer is like a poem, then a song, then a desperate plea.

Our Father,
Who art in heaven,
hallowed be Thy name;
Thy kingdom come;
Thy will be done on earth as it is in heaven.
Give us this day our daily bread
and forgive us our trespasses as we forgive those
who trespass against us

and lead us not into temptation,
but deliver us from evil.

Padre nuestro que estás en el cielo
santificado sea tu nombre.
Vénganos en tu rieno.
Hágase tu voluntad
así en la tierra como en el cielo.
Danos hoy el pan de cada dia
Y perdona nuestras ofensas así como
nosotros perdonamos a los que nos ofenden.
No nos dejes caer en tentación
y líbranos de todo mal, amen.

A soft light envelops MONICA and HELENA.

(Enter ASUNCION in military clothes and carrying
a machine gun. She is a brunette, hair combed back into a
pony tail, and wears make-up)

ASUNCION

(Examines the women on their cots and
starts prodding HELENA)

Wake up, sleeping beauty! COMANDANTE wants to see you.

(MONICA sits up and rubs her eyes)

MONICA

I'm coming, just a minute.

Act 1, Scene One

ASUNCION

(Continues prodding HELENA)

Not YOU, he wants this one.

HELENA

Hey, stop it! I heard you.

(Sits up)

What time is it? What the hell do you want?

ASUNCION

COMANDANTE wants to see you.

(A gunshot is heard close by)

HELENA

THIS IS A TRICK! I'M NOT COMING! NO!! NO!!!

(ASUNCION pulls HELENA out of bed)

HELP! HELP!

ASUNCION

(Slaps her)

SHUT UP OR I'LL BLOW YOUR HEAD OFF!!

(Grabs HELENA'S arm and takes her away)

BLACKOUT

the Backroom

4

Scene Two

*Same room, barely lit. MONICA lies on the floor with
ASUNCION on top of her, a machine gun squeezed between
them. At first the women struggle, but it is clear that the
machine gun may go off.*

ASUNCION

You'll get that peaceful look of the dead.

MONICA

Do YOU want to die?

ASUNCION

LISTEN TO ME! You'll feel a dull pain before your soul
goes to HELL.

MONICA

But,

*(ASUNCION squeezes the trigger and both women end up in a
pool of blood. MONICA raises her hand to touch her left side)*

BLACKOUT

6

Scene Three

MONICA and HELENA sit on the floor smoking a cigarette.

MONICA

I quit smoking years ago.

HELENA

(Takes cigarette)

REALLY? Hard to tell, the way you're devouring my cigarette.

(Hands cigarette back to MONICA)

MONICA

(Inhales slowly, taking her time)

I never thought it could taste so good.

(Coughs)

HELENA

(Grabs cigarette)

Don't waste it. I had to give the guard my tweezers in exchange.

(Extinguishes cigarette and puts it in her pocket)

Let's save the rest for later.

MONICA

(Coughs)

You won't need tweezers here.

HELENA

I'M SICK OF BEING HERE!

MONICA

And where would you go? We're safer here than out there.

(Points to the jungle)

HELENA

You're right.

MONICA

Ironic, isn't it?

HELENA

We'll be dead when we leave this place.

MONICA

The army could liberate us.

HELENA

If the army gets involved we'll leave in a casket.

MONICA

A bag is more like it…I'm not afraid of death.

HELENA

Well, I'M not ready for it.

(Enter JUAN)

Act 1, Scene Three

JUAN

Atención! COMANDANTE is here to see you.

(Enter COMANDANTE, a handsome man with dark hair and a moustache. He is followed by ASUNCION. While COMANDANTE, MONICA and HELENA talk, JUAN stands by the door and ASUNCION searches the room)

COMANDANTE

Good morning ladies. I hope you are comfortable?

(Smells smoke)

Smoking is BAD for you.

MONICA

So is captivity.

HELENA

(To COMANDANTE)

Will you get us more cigarettes, PLEASE?

COMANDANTE

They'll ruin your health.

(To MONICA)

How's your cough?

MONICA

The same. This dampness doesn't help.

HELENA

(Walks closer to COMANDANTE)

Our future president smokes too, don't you, MONICA?

(To COMANDANTE)

There you have it. She has vices, just like you and me.

(JUAN stares at HELENA and smiles)

MONICA

There's not a great incentive to stop smoking while waiting for death.

COMANDANTE

It's all for a good cause.

MONICA

That depends on your perspective.

COMANDANTE

That IS my perspective.

MONICA

So you kidnap, torture and murder in order to liberate.

COMANDANTE

(To MONICA)

YOU of all people should understand.

MONICA

Why?

COMANDANTE

Because you want to change this country too.

MONICA

Peacefully.

COMANDANTE

How can you make peaceful changes after forty years of war?

HELENA

Good point!

MONICA

It IS possible.

COMANDANTE

People don't want to change.

(ASUNCION goes through MONICA'S and HELENA'S few belongings while the women glare at her. She glares back)

HELENA

COMANDANTE, could you get us a pack of Camel Lights? It's more fun to philosophize while you're smoking and drinking.

(Points to ASUNCION)

What's SHE looking for?

COMANDANTE

Routine search. I'll see what I can do, but if I get you anything, it'll be our *Nacionales*.

(MONICA and COMANDANTE look at each other)

MONICA

(To COMANDANTE)

How long do you plan to keep us here?

COMANDANTE

A couple of days. The paramilitary is on our heels.

(Walks closer to MONICA)

Is there ANYTHING I can do for you?

HELENA

You sound like the manager of a five-star hotel.

COMANDANTE

Fill out a satisfaction survey before you leave.

(As COMANDANTE and GUARDS exit,
ASUNCION looks at MONICA menacingly while
JUAN smiles at HELENA)

MONICA

If we're not in a bag.

HELENA

Isn't he irresistible?

MONICA

What?

HELENA

I like his dark eyes, his deep voice, the way he carries himself; he has class…Come on! Don't tell me he's not handsome.

MONICA

AGUJA is not my type, but there's something about him, a certain charm.

HELENA

It's charisma.

Act 1, Scene Three

MONICA

Don't forget he's a murderer …

HELENA

(Checks under her pillow for something)

Who hides it well…very cunning.

MONICA

What do you know about the BACK ROOM?

HELENA

It's always locked. COMANDANTE keeps the key in a separate key chain in his pocket. No one knows what's inside. I've seen the door, even tried the knob, but it didn't work. When I turned around COMANDANTE was standing behind me. *I wouldn't push my luck,* he said. Scary. There's a strange smell coming from the room. I wonder if he keeps corpses in there.

MONICA

(Covers her face)

That's disgusting!

HELENA

I noticed the way you look at him.

MONICA

I wonder why he came to talk to us.

HELENA

He's been observing us with his binoculars. Haven't you noticed?

MONICA

No.

HELENA

I'll point him out next time.

MONICA

Why does he spy on us?

*(Enter JUAN. He calls HELENA to the side,
pulls a pair of tweezers out of his pocket and whispers in her ear.
HELENA demonstrates how they work. JUAN exits)*

MONICA

What did he want?

HELENA

To find out how the tweezers work.

MONICA

What on earth does he want tweezers for?

HELENA

His girlfriend.

MONICA

Is she a rebel?

HELENA

No. She lives in a village twenty miles from here.

MONICA

Poor girl.

HELENA

(Runs to call JUAN)

Wait! JUAN! Come back! I need to ask you something.

(Enter JUAN)

Act 1, Scene Three

JUAN

What is it?

HELENA

Have you ever been in the BACK ROOM?

MONICA

What's this all about?

HELENA

(To MONICA)

Haven't YOU ever heard of the BACK ROOM?

JUAN

NO ONE is allowed in there.

HELENA

Aren't YOU curious?

JUAN

Not enough to risk my life! The last prisoner who broke in was shot on the spot. Another one lost his tongue.

MONICA

RUMORS!

HELENA

That's GROSS! Does ANYONE know what's in there?

JUAN

(Shrugs)

We're not allowed near when COMANDANTE unlocks the door.

HELENA

Could it be arms or drugs?

JUAN

Those are in our warehouse. Don't EVER mention the
BACK ROOM to COMANDANTE AGUJA.

(JUAN exits)

MONICA

WERE YOU TRYING TO GET US KILLED?

HELENA

Just wanted to know. Boy, you're a good liar! You would
make a fine president!

(Stretches and starts pacing)

16

I'm so stiff! Can't even touch my toes!

(Touches her toes then bounces up)

MONICA

Don't bounce like that! You could hurt yourself. I'll teach
you yoga.

(Starts stretching)

HELENA

I don't need YOU to teach ME anything.

MONICA

What did the guard say?

HELENA

Nothing.

Act 1, Scene Three

MONICA

I know he gives you information.

(Sits on the floor and stretches)

Last night I dreamed that ASUNCION was on top of me, her machine gun resting on my ribs. It's the moment I've dreaded ever since I got here, but I wasn't afraid. I could hear but I couldn't talk. It was like swimming underwater.

HELENA

That woman hates you... She's dangerous.

(A gunshot is heard. HELENA jumps)

What was that?

MONICA

Our wake-up call. Breakfast will be here any minute.

HELENA

Aren't you scared?

MONICA

What difference does it make?

HELENA

I'm so damn tired of walking! Look at my feet.

(Shows MONICA her feet)

They're full of sores. I'll never fit into my shoes again.

MONICA

They'll heal. But these mosquito bites...

(Pulls shirt sleeve up)

will never heal. They'll leave scars.

HELENA

I hate the jungle! People sit in their homes sipping cocktails and talking about the environment and the rain forest; but they have running water and electricity. I'd like to see them here!

MONICA

They're right. We're ruining the earth by tearing thousands of trees down every day.

HELENA

Poor mother earth! What ungrateful children we are. I forgot you were a candidate for the green party.

MONICA

Did you see that Anaconda by the river yesterday?

HELENA

(Smells her clothes)

I can't stand this smell! I'm not talking about sweat. I'm talking about the humidity in the air. It stinks.

MONICA

Did you ever hear of Saint Magnolia? When the inquisition burnt her, the scent of magnolia filled the air.

HELENA

Are you making this up, or did you go to Catholic school?

MONICA

Sacred Heart.

HELENA

It must be awful to be burnt alive.

Act 1, Scene Three

MONICA

How would YOU like to die?

HELENA

When I think about death I feel nausea. Last year the
National Liberation Army threatened to blow the TV
station up. My colleagues hired bodyguards
but I dyed my hair blond. The chief suggested a face lift!

MONICA

(Looks at HELENA closely)

You don't have many wrinkles. I've seen some real monsters
delivering the evening news.

HELENA

He also said I should hem my skirts a little higher!

MONICA

Did you?

HELENA

(Feels around her face for wrinkles)

I went on a diet and discovered YOU. Thought we could
show THEM all. The chauvinistic pigs in this country, the
Barbie dolls eating the screen up with their eyes and FAT
lips. Now I rot in this hole, all because I wanted to do
something important.

MONICA

What about me? I thought I'd be doing something
worthwhile for this country, and I'm rotting away too.

(Pause)

Did you like reporting on war?

HELENA

War gets old after a few months. I like fashion; it gives us a sense of beauty, makes us focus on the present.

MONICA

I knew a famous designer in Rome.

HELENA

Who?

MONICA

Valentino. He designed my wedding gown.

HELENA

Oh my God!!

(Stands up, ties her shirt in front, pulls her pants and starts strutting around the room like a model)

I would give ANYTHING to wear an original Valentino! I don't care if it's a swimsuit.

MONICA

I can't picture ANYONE wearing one of his tiny suits.

HELENA

(Continues strutting)

Use your imagination! I could squeeze into a size four. Jealous?

MONICA

Jalousie means blind in French.

(Motions to HELENA that someone is listening)

Act 1, Scene Three

HELENA

(Walks closer to the door)

THINK OF SOMEONE SPYING BEHIND DOORS, AS THEY DO HERE.

(Footsteps are heard hurrying away; turns to MONICA)

She's gone. We better watch what we say.

MONICA

She'd like to see me dead.

HELENA

(Stops strutting in front of MONICA and studies her)

You look lonely.

MONICA

It's one thing to be lonely; it's another to be waiting for a death sentence.

HELENA

What do you care? You've had everything.

MONICA

Not everything.

HELENA

For instance?

MONICA

THIS is not what I wanted. I turned forty-two last week. I had plans…

HELENA

Such as?

MONICA

Teaching every child in this country to read by the age of ten. Getting rid of this…

(Pinches her stomach)

HELENA

P L E A S E spare me! In a couple more weeks you'll be skin and bones, begging for some fat.

MONICA

I wanted to be with my children, learn to play the piano and start painting again. I often hear piano music in my head.

('Satie's Gymnopedie' n. 1 plays)

HELENA

I didn't know you painted.

MONICA

I did, in Rome; studied Michelangelo's work at the Vatican until my parents signed me up at the university.

HELENA

Why did you major in Political Science?

MONICA

Mother wanted another politician in the family.

Act 1, Scene Three

HELENA

*(Takes a mirror out of her pocket, looks at herself
and passes her finger over her brows)*

You're right. What's the point of tweezing here?

(Shows MONICA her hands)

Look at these nails! I can't remember the last time I had a manicure. Every Saturday I used to go to a little beauty parlor around the corner from my house. They treated me like a celebrity.

MONICA

You ARE a celebrity! You're a reporter.

HELENA

I feel like a failure.

MONICA

Listen to us! We're in the jungle. We've lost track of time; don't know how much longer we'll live and we worry about broken nails. We must be going crazy!

HELENA

Thinking about death drives me crazy. Knowing I didn't have a choice drives me crazy.

MONICA

WHAT DO YOU MEAN YOU DIDN'T HAVE A CHOICE? You always do.

HELENA

I WAS KIDNAPPED!! Remember? YOU were desperate for votes and entered guerrilla territory even after the army warned you!

MONICA

I didn't know they would imprison me!

(Studies HELENA)

As a reporter, <u>YOU knew there was a risk.</u> That's what you journalists do for fame and money. Right? Get the news, risk your lives for that moment of glory!

HELENA

And YOU think politicians are any different?

MONICA

I planned to investigate the corruption in the government.

HELENA

EVERYONE knows about the bribes our last president took.

(Holds mirror in front of MONICA)

When are you going to admit that your political career is over? You're still campaigning.

MONICA

Why do you hate me? I didn't ask you to follow me around the country.

HELENA

(Looks at her nails)

I don't hate you. I hate your arrogance. After a privileged life in Rome you came back like Joan of Arc to save us! The world really doesn't like heroines, you know.

MONICA

(Gets close to HELENA, faces her)

<u>Why don't YOU leave me alone?</u>

Act 1, Scene Three

HELENA

<u>Because if it weren't for YOU, I wouldn't be here.</u> Every morning I remember that.

MONICA

Who told you to come snooping around? You were looking for your story and you found it.

HELENA

<u>Want a story?</u> ASUNCION told me COMANDANTE AGUJA plans to get rid of one of us before the New Year. Nothing personal, but I'll do everything I can to survive.

(Looks in the mirror again)

You could make my career.

MONICA

I don't talk to the press. Besides, EVERYONE knows my story.

HELENA

I'm talking about a biography that reveals what drives you, shows the public the REAL MONICA DELGADO weaknesses and all. I bet some things about you would shock your fans.

MONICA

(Walks over to HELENA)

IF WE EVER GET OUT OF HERE, I SWEAR I'LL…

*(ASUNCION enters as MONICA
and HELENA attack each other)*

ASUNCION

(Holds her machine gun up)

STOP IT, OR I'LL SHOOT YOU!

(Separates the women)

HELENA

IS THAT A PROMISE?

ASUNCION

(To HELENA)

COMANDANTE wants to see you.

(HELENA passes a hand through her hair, examines the tie in front of her shirt and pinches her cheeks. She puts her mirror in her pocket, glances at MONICA and exits with ASUNCION who glares at MONICA)

26

BLACKOUT

Scene Four

Same room. MONICA sits on the floor with her eyes closed.
She holds an orchid in her hand and inhales the aroma.
A Gregorian chant plays.

BLACKOUT

the Backroom

28

Scene Five

MONICA and COMANDANTE look at each other across a dimly lit room. She sits on a couch dressed in a sexy but sophisticated black dress and wears gold jewelry. He stands a few feet away with a drink in one hand and a spent cigar in the other. COMANDANTE looks the same except for a beard. The intensity of her gaze beckons him, and he walks toward her.

BLACKOUT

30

Scene Six

MONICA'S and HELENA'S room in the guerrilla camp.
MONICA continues sitting on the floor with her eyes closed and
the orchid in her hands. JUAN, ASUNCION and HELENA
enter. HELENA'S hair is combed. She has a glow about her.
She glances at MONICA and jingles a charm bracelet as she
walks by. MONICA keeps her eyes closed. HELENA lies on her
cot. The GUARDS stand by the door.

HELENA

(To MONICA)

Where did you get the orchid?

MONICA

It was on the table when I came back from laundry duty.
I had an admirer who used to send me orchids every year
on the anniversary of our first meeting. No matter what
part of the world I was in, a box of orchids would arrive.

(ASUNCION laughs)

HELENA

How romantic! I bet you were fantasizing about him.

MONICA

No, I was thinking about how ironic it is to have the orchid
as our national flower, since it represents purity and
spiritual perfection.

HELENA

Remember those silver orchids with rough emeralds in the middle for sale in tourist shops? They mean much more than purity.

JUAN

(Playful)

I didn't know.

HELENA

That's because you're out here in the jungle. If you ever come to the city, I'll show you around! You can buy one of those silver orchids for your mother. She'll love it.

JUAN

What else does it mean?

HELENA

You're a curious boy, aren't you? Let me just say it's erotic.

JUAN

What?

(ASUNCION laughs)

HELENA

I'll tell you later when we go hunting for orchids.

JUAN

They're everywhere.

(Voice on loud speakers)

FELIZ NAVIDAD COMPATRIOTAS. VIVA LA REVOLUCION!!!

Act 1, Scene Six

(Christmas music plays and both GUARDS stand by the door with their machine guns ready)

ASUNCION

(To JUAN)

IDIOTA. Why do you let them make fun of you like that?

MONICA

(To JUAN)

What day is it?

JUAN

Christmas Eve. IF IT WEREN'T FOR YOU, I'd be with my family tonight.

MONICA

I didn't tell you to become a guerrilla fighter. You should be in school.

(ASUNCION laughs)

Can you read and write?

JUAN

HA! THAT'S A GOOD ONE, LADY! There's no schools around here. I've already learned all I need to know.

MONICA

How long have you been with the rebels?

JUAN

Three years.

MONICA

Why did you join?

JUAN

EVER HEARD OF POVERTY? Do you know what it's like to be hungry all day?

(Glances at ASUNCION)

MONICA

Now I do.

JUAN

My old man disappeared when I was ten. Sometimes all we ate was a piece of bread. One day my old lady gave me shoe polish and a rag and told me to bring home some money. A big shot at the university took me to a meeting. I signed up.

(Pacing around the room)

34

I'm learning to read and write; I can shoot pretty well. My salary buys food and clothes for the family.

MONICA

Don't you miss them? Your mother?

JUAN

I do. We never had much of a Christmas, but we went to mass on Christmas Eve.

ASUNCION

Pobrecito…

MONICA

When was the last time they heard from you?

Act 1, Scene Six

JUAN

A year ago; we're not supposed to contact our families; if the paramilitary gets a whiff of our presence in a village, they'll kill everyone. They don't even bother to ask questions. <u>ASSASSINS</u>!

(Stops walking)

Maybe they think I'm dead. I wonder if they remember me.

MONICA

I would NEVER forget you. I would be praying for you tonight.

(Walks up to JUAN and embraces him)

ASUNCION

(Laughs)

¡Que tonto!

JUAN

I need more than "Our Father's" to survive.

MONICA

Prayer is important. Faith is important. We can't just sit here waiting to die.

HELENA

(Sits up on her cot. To MONICA)

I didn't know you were religious!

the Backroom

MONICA

I'm spiritual.

(To JUAN)

You look tired. Why don't you rest a minute?

*(JUAN grabs a chair and sits by the table
but does not put his machine gun down)*

You can put your gun down. We won't take it from you.

JUAN

(Glances at ASUNCION)

I'm not allowed.

(Places gun by the table)

HELENA

(To MONICA)

The nuns really did you in! Now you're talking about faith.

MONICA

I'm a Buddhist. Buddhism is more forgiving.

JUAN

What's that about?

ASUNCION

What do YOU care? We're all going to die!

HELENA

Karma and reincarnation.

(JUAN shakes his head)

Act 1, Scene Six

MONICA

Buddhists believe in many lives. Karma is the influence of our past actions on our present life. If you're suffering now, it's because of a past lifetime.

JUAN

I must've been a criminal. Do we come back with the same people?

MONICA

Yes. Maybe I was your mother in another lifetime.

HELENA

Or mine.

(ASUNCION laughs)

MONICA

I hope not!

JUAN

(Cleans his boots with his shirt sleeve)

HELENA

(To JUAN)

Do you like this better than shining shoes?

JUAN

<u>This</u> is my type of work. I shined shoes Monday through Sunday. One day a woman put her boot on my stool. Lady, I'd rather starve, I told her, than shine YOUR shoes.

*(Sits up and points his rifle at MONICA.
HELENA covers her face)*

MONICA

STOP THAT! You could hurt someone.

ASUNCION

That's the point. Isn't it?

(Raises her gun)

MONICA

Your leader, Father Perez. What was he like?

JUAN

Padrecito was the most intelligent man I ever laid eyes on; studied in Europe. Fought for this country, and like a whore she betrayed him. Got his throat cut a year after I joined.

MONICA

You've learned your lessons well. I bet you're a good student.

ASUNCION

BUT YOU AREN'T! Even the gringos never had a woman president.

MONICA

Where did you hear that?

JUAN

From COMANDANTE AGUJA. He knows everything. He's traveled.

Act 1, Scene Six

MONICA

I wouldn't believe EVERYTHING COMANDANTE
AGUJA tells you. He's just a man.

*(A gunshot rings close by. JUAN, HELENA and MONICA
look at each other. ASUNCION receives a call on her
walkie-talkie. She points her machine gun first at
MONICA and then at HELENA and exits.
Footsteps and muffled voices are heard. JUAN stands up, grabs
his machine gun and starts walking out.
MONICA approaches him and places her hand on his shoulder.
She strokes his head)*

JUAN

We have a meeting.

*(Starts walking away but HELENA
grabs him by his shirt sleeve)*

HELENA

Wait! Do you ever worry about the army catching up with
you?

JUAN

(Stops)

Those bastards are pathetic! They can't move very fast; their
boots are too big.

MONICA

You're kidding!

JUAN

No. The gringos sold their old boots and uniforms to our army. Haven't you ever seen Independence Day Parade? Our soldiers look like clowns in those big boots. Everybody knows the gringos have huge feet!

(Turns to exit)

HELENA

JUAN, where are we?

JUAN

Central unit number thirty-six.

MONICA

Is this where the guerrilla has its headquarters?

JUAN

We don't have headquarters. It's COMANDANTE AGUJA'S hideout.

(JUAN exits)

MONICA

(To HELENA)

How long have I been here?

HELENA

(Studies her bracelet)

How should I know?

MONICA

I thought your job was to chronicle my life and death.

Act 1, Scene Six

HELENA

I have better things to do now, like <u>trying to save my own skin!</u>

MONICA

When did you come?

HELENA

(Pulls a neatly folded piece of newspaper from one of her shirt pockets, looks at the date)

Four months ago. You had been here about six weeks.

MONICA

You know what they say…

HELENA

What?

MONICA

That after six months you're dead.

HELENA

That's what THEY say. But YOU could prove them wrong.

(Puts piece of paper back in her pocket and goes back to studying her bracelet)

Were things around here the same before I came? Or have they changed?

MONICA

They've changed.

HELENA

In what way?

MONICA

What did COMANDANTE want from you?

HELENA

To give me a present.

MONICA

Oh.

HELENA

*(Walks over to MONICA and dangles her wrist
in front of her to show off the bracelet)*

Eighteen karat. Isn't it BEAUTIFUL? Look at these jewels.

(Shows MONICA the charms)

There's a windmill, a little cross, a bull and a coin. I love the emerald on the clasp! If I die, you'll get it.

MONICA

(Pretends not to hear)

You were gone awhile.

HELENA

I never rush him. I have time.

MONICA

We ALL have time. Do you like seeing him?

HELENA

He's fun.

*(Pretends to examine the bracelet. Tries to
show it to MONICA)*

You're not envious, are you?

42

Act 1, Scene Six

MONICA

Don't be ridiculous!

(Pushes HELENA'S arm away)

Doesn't it bother you that your bracelet belonged to someone who is now dead?

HELENA

I'm still alive and I'm enjoying it. Why not? What happened to your Rolex?

MONICA

How did you know I had a Rolex?

HELENA

I saw it in your picture in a magazine.

MONICA

They took it from me.

HELENA

Do you want me to try and get it back for you?

MONICA

I could care less what time it is.

HELENA

I heard your Rolex was all you wore to bed.

MONICA

That's a lie!

(Walks over to the table and sits down)

(Enter ASUNCION)

ASUNCION

GET READY TO CLIMB!

HELENA

But we just had a drill! Where are we going?

ASUNCION

(Points machine gun at them)

COME ON! MOVE IT!

BLACKOUT

44

Scene Seven

The jungle. The GUARDS are leading MONICA and HELENA up a mountain. Both women are blindfolded. They're dragging their feet. Initially it's dark but then the sun rises.

MONICA

How long have we been walking?

ASUNCION

SHUT UP!

HELENA

At least five hours. Let's stop to rest. How many drills have we done this week?

JUAN

(Pokes HELENA with the machine gun)

You'll stop when I tell you.

HELENA

What happened to Mr. Nice Guy?

(To MONICA)

Is this the sweet boy you felt sorry for?

MONICA

He's doing his job.

(To JUAN)

Listen, I have to rest for five minutes. Can we take the blindfolds off?

JUAN

(Stops, takes blindfolds off)

If the army ever finds us, you'll have to run through this jungle.

*(Sits on a rock, puts machine gun down
and wipes his forehead)*

ASUNCION

Time to head back. Pretty soon the bugs will eat us alive.

(Sun starts rising)

MONICA

(Observes the sunrise)

That's magnificent! I see the Andes in the distance. They pierce the sky. Look at the snow on their peaks!

(Takes a deep breath)

Ah, the air up here is so thin.

(Coughs)

JUAN

Breathe slow, you could get dizzy. Your lungs are not strong.

46

Act 1, Scene Seven

HELENA

(Takes a deep breath, turns to JUAN)

Do you have a cigarette?

JUAN

(Starts looking through his pockets)

No. I gave you my last smoke.

HELENA

*(Searches in her pocket, finds the half smoked cigarette;
to JUAN)*

Here it is! Do you have a light?

MONICA

That's poison. This is the cleanest air we'll ever breathe.

ASUNCION

If it were up to me, YOU wouldn't be breathing at all!

HELENA

On my tombstone they'll write "she died of a bullet hole in her head with fresh air in her lungs."

JUAN

(To HELENA)

You're really something!

HELENA

Do you think so?

JUAN

Yeah, if I didn't have a girlfriend…

ASUNCION

Only one?

HELENA

(Touches his hand)

But I'm so much older than you! Of course, there's a lot I could teach you.

ASUNCION

You're pathetic!

(Footsteps are heard)

JUAN

FOLLOW ME!

(Starts running; MONICA and HELENA look at each other and hesitate for a minute but ASUNCION points her machine gun at them)

JUAN

FOLLOW ME I SAID!

BLACKOUT

Scene Eight

MONICA and HELENA are sitting on a rock on the mountain. The GUARDS sit on the ground next to them. They pass a flask of water around.

JUAN

If the army finds us, don't surrender. Just run. Those bastards can kill!

(Notices an exotic butterfly close to him, takes it and offers it to HELENA)

A present for you! Some people would pay a lot for this. Collectors, they call them. I know one who comes here every year.

HELENA

He must be crazy risking his life for a butterfly.

JUAN

We give him coca too.

HELENA

Get it away from me!

ASUNCION

You want me to kill it?

MONICA

DON'T. Its life is short enough.

JUAN

(Studies butterfly)

Who would pin a butterfly in a glass case?

HELENA

What's the difference between her and us? We're prisoners too.

MONICA

Look at the colors on her wings! They're beautiful. Set it free.

ASUNCION

(Pokes the butterfly. It remains still)

It's dead.

50

HELENA

Killed by your sweet touch.

JUAN

(Places the butterfly on the ground. Receives a call on his walkie-talkie)

Sí hermano, llegamos.

*(The GUARDS walk away to talk.
MONICA studies the butterfly)*

HELENA

I hope COMANDANTE sends for me tonight.

MONICA

You enjoy spending time with a killer?

Act 1, Scene Eight

HELENA

When I'm with him, he's a fascinating, witty man. We have a drink, smoke cigars and talk about world politics. He's very knowledgeable.

MONICA

Is that all you do? Smoke and talk?

HELENA

Oh no, we do a lot more than that! I only wish he'd take his boots off.

(Cleans dirt off of her boots with a stick)

The other day we talked about you.

MONICA

Really?

HELENA

He said you're arrogant.

MONICA

HOW CAN HE SAY THAT?

HELENA

I told him you're just a little uptight.

MONICA

GREAT!

HELENA

Give him a chance.

MONICA

WHY SHOULD I GIVE HIM A CHANCE? It's not like he's given ME one.

HELENA

You expect special treatment?

MONICA

(Drinks water)

I'm already getting special treatment. The same one you are.

HELENA

(Takes flask away from MONICA)

COMANDANTE would tell me.

MONICA

What makes you think that?

HELENA

Lovers share secrets.

MONICA

You're a reporter!

HELENA

Even my pen is gone.

MONICA

You gave up your last pen? What about your story?

HELENA

I don't give a damn about it anymore! I can't be objective.

MONICA

No one is ever objective.

(Glances over at JUAN who is walking back)

JUAN

I'm using your pen to write a love letter.

HELENA

For me, or for your girlfriend?

JUAN

For you of course! My girlfriend can't read.

HELENA

I'll help you practice your writing.

(ASUNCION joins them)

JUAN

When you're not busy with COMANDANTE?

HELENA

I can't very well say no to him.

ASUNCION

(Points at MONICA)

She did!

(Takes flask and drinks)

HELENA

What do you mean?

MONICA

I don't know what you're talking about.

ASUNCION

Yes you do! You haven't told your FRIEND?

HELENA

What?

(JUAN tells ASUNCION to be quiet but she ignores him)

ASUNCION

(To HELENA)

Before you came, COMANDANTE used to send for her.

(Points at MONICA with her machine gun)

HELENA

That's impossible! He would've told me!

JUAN

(To MONICA)

54

Tell her, tell her the truth.

BLACKOUT

Scene Nine

Midnight. While it is still dark, we hear bells chiming. Lights illuminate MONICA and COMANDANTE AGUJA on opposite ends of the stage. On the left, AGUJA is in bed reading a letter. He stops reading, turns to his night table, takes MONICA'S picture out of the drawer and looks at it longingly. On the opposite side of the stage Monica is in bed staring at the ceiling. She picks up an orchid resting on her pillow and inhales its aroma, daydreaming.

BLACKOUT

56

Scene Ten

Same room. MONICA sits on her cot, legs gathered to her chest, head resting on knees. 'Satie's Gymnopedie' n. 1 plays. HELENA enters, walks up to the table, takes a chair.

MONICA

What did AGUJA say?

HELENA

He wanted to give me the latest news.

> *(Stands up, changes demeanor to resemble that of a television reporter; pretends to hold a microphone, alters her voice)*

Yesterday two of COMANDANTE AGUJA'S hostages parked car bombs near the Church of Our Holy Trinity killing hundreds and injuring thousands. The church doors were blown to bits and pedestrians rushed in to seek refuge. AGUJA expressed regret concerning the damages to the church and the loss of lives. *Until the government decides to cooperate, we'll be forced to continue with our offensive,* he added. The rebels plan to shoot a video of MONICA DELGADO, former presidential candidate, reading COMANDANTE AGUJA'S requests to the government. Senator ALICIA GUTIERREZ will be executed tonight. When asked why he chose to sacrifice GUTIERREZ and not DELGADO or her cellmate MAYO, the guerrilla leader replied *they're worth more alive than dead.*

the Backroom

*(Mockingly, in a man's voice, pretending to
stroke an imaginary moustache)*

*Gutierrez's execution is my Christmas gift to the country.
I'm getting rid of one more dirty politician.*

*(MONICA and HELENA laugh but soon grow silent.
ASUNCION arrives and stands by the door
at the usual spot. She cleans her nails while listening to the
conversation, her machine gun by her side)*

MONICA

You have a good rapport with the camera.

HELENA

I get nervous every time.

(Puts imaginary microphone down)

COMANDANTE has connections in one of the local
channels; he promised he would try to get me in there.

MONICA

I wouldn't trust him.

HELENA

Who am I supposed to trust, then?

MONICA

I can't believe he plans to execute SENATOR
GUTIERREZ!!

HELENA

Better her than us.

Act 1, Scene Ten

MONICA

I'll be next.

HELENA

No. I will.

(Embraces MONICA; both women cry)

ASUNCION

Pobrecitas…

HELENA

Self-pity won't save us.

MONICA

(Wiping her tears)

I miss my children.

HELENA

Where are they?

MONICA

In New Zealand with their father. Thank God they're far away from this hole.

(Glances at ASUNCION)

ASUNCION

How patriotic!

(Receives a call on her walkie-talkie and leaves)

HELENA

(Walks over to her cot, grabs a bottle of aguardiente from under her pillow and carries it over to the table)

I thought you loved your country! Here, have some.

(Hands MONICA the bottle of aguardiente)

MONICA

My love is not reciprocated. Where did you get this?

(Takes a sip, shuts her eyes, swallows and coughs)

HELENA

From JUAN. I gave him my last pair of panty hose. I hated giving them up, even if they were full of holes. He insisted on watching me while I took them off. He's obsessed with me!

MONICA

Has he ever touched you?

HELENA

He knows he can.

MONICA

Come on, he's still a child.

HELENA

I'll try to remember that the next time he points his Kalashnikov at me.

MONICA

The boy is scared, like all of us. If you continue flirting with him…

Act 1, Scene Ten

HELENA

Oh, come off it Mother Teresa!

(MONICA and HELENA pass the bottle back and forth)

MONICA

He's better than ASUNCION. That woman gives me the creeps. Sometimes she looks at me like she's going to shoot me.

HELENA

She would, if she could get away with it.

MONICA

I'm so cold!

(Rubs her arms)

HELENA

Where did you live in Rome?

MONICA

A block from the Spanish Steps.

HELENA

Close to that famous hotel, the one where all the celebrities hang out?

MONICA

The Hassler? We had cocktails there once a week.

(Paces around the room)

I got tired of celebrities. You know what I miss? Watching the sun go down from my terrace while sipping Chianti.

HELENA

(Takes bottle and drinks)

What's Rome like?

MONICA

Imagine being able to pray in a different church every day until you die.

HELENA

It's too late to pray. Pass the *aguardiente*!

(Takes bottle, drinks and smacks her lips)

If I ever get out of here, I swear I'll visit Rome.

MONICA

Go in May.

(GUARDS enter carrying trays with two plates of rice, a water jar and two glasses. They walk up to the table and put the trays down)

ASUNCION

Lunch is served! It's not spaghetti, but you're lucky to get any food at all!

HELENA

You've been eavesdropping again. Did you bring us forks this time, or are we expected to eat this shit with our hands?

Act 1, Scene Ten

JUAN

The lady is in a bad mood. You're in luck.

*(Pulls two forks out of his shirt pocket
and hands them to HELENA and MONICA)*

This will cost you.

MONICA

Just add it to the list. Did you make sure the water was boiled this time?

ASUNCION

Yes, YOUR MAJESTY.

*(JUAN pours them each a glass of water.
HELENA and MONICA take their plates and
start eating halfheartedly)*

HELENA

(Throws her plate on the floor)

THIS IS DISGUSTING! THERE'S A SCORPION IN MY FOOD!

ASUNCION

CLEAN IT UP! COME GET THE PAIL!

*(HELENA tries to speak but ASUNCION points the gun at
her and both women exit. JUAN sits down)*

JUAN

(To MONICA)

Your friend gets on my nerves.

MONICA

And yours wants to kill me. Is something bothering you?

(JUAN moves in his chair)

What is it? Maybe I can help you.

JUAN

Lady, you can't even help yourself! Only God can help me.

(Pause)

Soon I'll be a father.

MONICA

You're too young!

JUAN

I'm old enough to hold a gun and kill. Have you seen the way your friend looks at me?

MONICA

Don't pay any attention to her; she's just going through a midlife crisis. What are you going to do?

JUAN

Is she THAT old?

MONICA

She's over twenty-five and worried about it. Answer my question.

JUAN

I don't know.

MONICA

How old is your girl?

Act 1, Scene Ten

JUAN

My age.

(Touches his stomach)

Oh, I almost forgot! I have something for you.

*(Pulls a book out from under his shirt,
looks around to make sure no one is watching and hands it to
MONICA; she takes the book and reads the title)*

MONICA

Autobiography of a Tibetan Monk by Palden Gyatso. I've
never read it.

JUAN

It has too many big words. COMANDANTE AGUJA
sent it to you. I told him about our conversation the other
day. Keep it hidden.

*(HELENA enters with pail and rags.
MONICA hides the book under her shirt.
HELENA gets on her knees and starts cleaning up.
She moves close to JUAN.
Her shirt is unbuttoned. MONICA notices)*

MONICA

(To JUAN)

Next time bring paper and pencil. I'll teach you some big
words.

(JUAN exits)

HELENA

*(Hums for a minute, then puts the rags in the pail
and moves it to the side)*

You have a crush on him too?

MONICA

Your blouse is unbuttoned.

HELENA

(Looks down at her chest and starts buttoning up her blouse)

I hadn't noticed! I'm hungry.

MONICA

(Hands HELENA her plate)

You can have mine.

HELENA

You didn't eat anything.

*(MONICA stands up and drops the book. She tries to
pick it up but HELENA grabs it first and starts
reading the back cover)*

*Gyatso endured interrogation and torture for the strength of his
beliefs.* Where did you get it?

MONICA

I exchanged my Rolex for it.

HELENA

You REALLY are a liar! And you kept it hidden all this time?

MONICA

I didn't want it to be taken from me.

Act 1, Scene Ten

HELENA

What is it about?

MONICA

The Chinese reform in Tibet after the 1950 invasion.
Those poor Tibetans have suffered, just like us.

HELENA

But WE weren't invaded by another country.

MONICA

That's right. We're being terrorized by our own people.

*(HELENA starts eating while MONICA
peruses the book)*

HELENA

I can't eat this shit.

(Pushes the plate away, takes a drink of aguardiente)

MONICA

Don't let the ASUNCION hear you.

HELENA

What did you have for breakfast in Rome?

MONICA

My favorite was a cappuccino and an apricot filled brioche.
Hmm, sometimes the warm apricot marmalade burnt my
tongue.

(Starts rubbing her hands)

I would give anything for a cappuccino right now.

HELENA

A plain cup of coffee with sugar would be enough for me, as long as it didn't taste like dirty water.

(Another shot is heard followed by a scream. HELENA and MONICA look at each other. MONICA lowers her head. Trying to sound cheerful)

What was your favorite Italian dish?

MONICA

(Stands up, picks up a rag, places it on her arm to resemble a waiter and speaks with an italian accent)

Welcome to Rome, Signorina, what shall you have today? A little wine?

(Pours aguardiente for HELENA. She drinks)

Il piatto del giorno is pasta with the seven ps. Delicious!

(Kisses her fingers)

(A shot is heard close by followed by screams. The women try to ignore it)

HELENA

(Playing along)

I'm famished. What does it have?

MONICA

Hot peppers, porcini, pepper, *panna* (which means cream), pancetta, tomatoes, I can't remember the last ingredient, oh yes! *Piselli*, peas.

HELENA

How do you make it?

Act 1, Scene Ten

MONICA

Giuseppe, he put olive oil in a pot.

HELENA

Then what?

MONICA

Add garlic and pancetta his beautiful wife cut; when that's cooked, stir in the cream and the porcini mushrooms; add cooked peas at the end before the hot peppers. I bring you that with spaghetti al dente and parmigiano cheese and you love me forever.

HELENA

Hmm. I'm hungry. How about a little amore after lunch? Or do you have to serve other starving tourists who are looking for good food and good love?

MONICA

Bella, we always have time for a little amore between the pasta and the second course!

(Both women grow silent. MONICA joins HELENA at the table, pours herself a drink, drinks)

HELENA

My stomach is grumbling. I wish we had some hot chocolate and bread.

MONICA

Sometimes I dream about warm, cheese filled *almojabanas* and hot chocolate.

HELENA

Right now I would confess to any crime for a basket of soft, chewy *pandeyucas*.

MONICA

Every summer when I visited my family, I would ask our driver to take me to the north to eat all the *pandeyucas* and *almojabanas* I wanted.

(Empties her glass)

You can live in another country for a thousand years and still miss the simplest things from your own.

HELENA

Now the truth comes out! You didn't move back here to save your country. You wanted to eat bread.

MONICA

Yes. Give us this day our daily bread. What I didn't expect to find was the cruelty, the indifference.

HELENA

(Pours more aguardiente in her glass and MONICA'S)

What was it like to be married to an Italian?

MONICA

I got tired of diplomats' wives and embassy parties. Then during one of my visits here I realized that my identity is closely tied to my culture, my country, and my language and I need a man who can understand this. MASSIMILIANO told me I was crazy when I decided to move back here.

HELENA

M A S S I M I L I A N O sounds like such an important name.

MONICA

His grandfather was a duke.

70

The role of culture in a marriage

Act 1, Scene Ten

HELENA

Nobility no less! He looks like Julio Iglesias.

MONICA

He's handsome, like my son.

(ASUNCION returns to her post)

HELENA

What about your kids?

MONICA

Beatrice is fifteen and Lorenzo ten. They lived with me until the kidnapping threats became unbearable.

HELENA

So you sent them to their father.

MONICA

Yes. I worry about Beatrice.

HELENA

Why?

MONICA

She refused to say goodbye to me.

HELENA

It has to be difficult growing up without her mother.

(Drinks)

MONICA

Hey, I'm still alive!

(Drinks)

*(ASUNCION enters, points machine gun
at MONICA)*

ASUNCION

Not for long!

MONICA

(Pushes gun away. To HELENA)

Have YOU ever been married?

(ASUNCION starts searching the room)

HELENA

I'm not cut out for marriage. I miss not having kids, though.

MONICA

A reporter's life is hectic. You wouldn't have time for them.

HELENA

YOU managed.

MONICA

(Walks over to her cot, lays down and stares at the ceiling)

Do you travel much?

(ASUNCION spots aguardiente, takes a drink)

HELENA

I went to Miami to learn English.

Act 1, Scene Ten

MONICA

Isn't Spanish the official language over there?

HELENA

I never learned English.

MONICA

What did you do during your free time?

HELENA

I watched television; saw the strangest things.

MONICA

Such as?

HELENA

The gringos seem to have a pill for everything.

(To ASUNCION)

What the hell are you looking for?

MONICA

I wish I had a pill right now.

HELENA

For headaches?

MONICA

For chills, pain, heartache.

(Crosses her legs)

HELENA

Sex too?

MONICA

I don't care about sex; I'm numb.

(A shot is heard, followed by screams.
MONICA jumps. ASUNCION laughs,
points gun at MONICA)

HELENA

Are European women different from us?

MONICA

Yes. They care about other things besides pleasing their men.

ASUNCION

What do YOU know?

HELENA

We have our feminists too!

MONICA

Where are they?

HELENA

Look at you, a presidential candidate.

MONICA

Yes. Look at me now.

ASUNCION

¡Pobrecita!

(Exits, laughing)

HELENA

(Takes out her mirror and looks at herself)

I've aged since I've been here.

Act 1, Scene Ten

MONICA

Don't be ridiculous.

HELENA

(Touches her forehead)

I see wrinkles I'd never noticed.

> *(MONICA walks over to the table, drinks from her glass and ignores HELENA)*

I can't figure out what MASSIMILIANO CONTI sees in you. Don't get me wrong. I think you're attractive, sensuous. You have class. But you are no Salma Hayek.

> *(HELENA walks over to MONICA and faces her)*

And yet, you've had a guerrilla leader for a lover and MASSIMILIANO CONTI—one of the most desirable men in the world—for a husband. Who is your secret love now? WHAT is your secret?

(Drinks)

MONICA

My brain.

HELENA

I have a brain too.

MONICA

Seriously, have you heard of CARMENCITA?

HELENA

The singer? Yes. She wears too much make-up.

MONICA

She's a middle-aged woman afraid of growing old. Have you noticed the way she dresses?

HELENA

You mean undresses?

MONICA

Yes. You've seen her videos. She takes her clothes off in front of the camera.

HELENA

She's competing with younger women. Some sing in their underwear and slither in the mud.

MONICA

How can they expect to be taken seriously?

HELENA

They're selling sex.

MONICA

Do you know why? Because they can't sing.

HELENA

Speaking of sex, Americans have strange ideas about it.

MONICA

Such as?

HELENA

You see it everywhere, on MTV, at the movies, in books and magazines. But you never talk about it. The gringos are repressed voyeurs.

Act 1, Scene Ten

MONICA

I agree. It's their puritan background. Unfortunately, we resemble them more every day.

HELENA

I'm hungry.

MONICA

Sex, like a good meal, should not be rushed. Sometimes Americans are in such a hurry, they eat in their cars.

HELENA

Do they have sex in their cars too?

MONICA

They do EVERYTHING in their cars. That's why they have such big cars; they like to drive long distances and to get there fast. But speed is desire's worst enemy.

HELENA

Americans watch sex on TV for hours.

MONICA

And make love for minutes.

HELENA

I wonder if they make love at all. They look so busy all the time.

MONICA

It's a process of consuming rather than enjoying.

HELENA

No wonder they have problems.

MONICA

Many end up in therapy or have to read a manual; I heard that now they watch a show called Dr. Phils. He seems to be the American version of a modern day shaman, helping heal the country.

HELENA

My next boyfriend will be Italian.

MONICA

(Studies HELENA for a minute)

You'll have to put on a little weight. Italians like real women.

HELENA

EXCUSE ME? I SUFFERED SO I COULD LOOK LIKE THIS!

(Puts her hands on her hips and stares at MONICA)

When are you going to tell me about COMANDANTE?

MONICA

Ask him.

HELENA

He won't talk. I'll just have to speculate about it in your bio.

MONICA

YOU could end up dead. COMANDANTE doesn't like that type of publicity.

HELENA

And YOU'RE are not front page news anymore.

(Takes another sip of aguardiente)

Act 1, Scene Ten

MONICA

(Stands in front of HELENA and mimicks her)

YOU have your eye on COMANDANTE. Isn't it a little mercenary?

HELENA

HE made a pass at me first. You can't expect him to stop living just because he's stuck in the middle of the jungle.

MONICA

YOU'RE LYING! YOU ARE NOT HIS TYPE!

HELENA

I HAVE BECOME HIS TYPE! He NEVER disappoints me. Whatever went on between you and COMANDANTE, he has made a choice. I wouldn't be surprised if he kills you instead of me.

MONICA

(Covers her ears and starts screaming)

I DON'T WANT TO HEAR YOUR LIES!!!

(HELENA laughs and MONICA grabs her by her hair. HELENA retaliates. Enter ASUNCION)

ASUNCION

(Throws MONICA a plastic bag full of clothes)

STOP IT!! COMANDANTE is expecting you for Christmas dinner in an hour; he wants you to dress up. Get ready. DON'T MAKE HIM WAIT.

BLACKOUT

the Backroom

80

Act 2
Scene One

The COMANDANTE'S barracks. A table has been set for three. Two candles adorn it. A bottle of aguardiente has been opened and a glass, half full, rests on the table next to a bowl of mangos and some canned sardines. Another bottle of aguardiente remains unopened at the opposite end of the table. An orchid rests by one of the dinner plates. There is a bookshelf with a stereo and compact disks on one side and books and a tarot deck on the other. The bottom of the shelf contains machine guns. At the opposite end of the stage stands a red door with a scrim behind it. HELENA and MONICA are in front of the table waiting for AGUJA. They wear skirts, blouses and high-heeled shoes. Their hair is combed. MONICA holds the plastic bag ASUNCION gave her. HELENA takes a sip from the glass on the table; she offers it to MONICA.

MONICA

Leave that! It's his.

HELENA

(Examines MONICA with a critical eye)

Do you really think COMANDANTE plans to choose one of us?

MONICA

No. It's a ploy to scare us. Remember, he said we're worth more alive than dead.

HELENA

I'm really scared.

(Takes another sip from the drink)

There's something I've been meaning to tell you.

MONICA

What?

HELENA

A strange need for confession before dying.

MONICA

Except I'm not a priest and you're not dying.

HELENA

I have a daughter.

MONICA

Where is she?

HELENA

In boarding school in England.

MONICA

How old is she?

HELENA

Twelve.

MONICA

When was the last time you saw her?

HELENA

Four years ago.

Act 2, Scene One

MONICA

And her father?

HELENA

Married; ran out on me when he found out I was pregnant. The sort of scandal that could destroy a career. I've been thinking… if I don't make it, would you go see her?

MONICA

You'll make it.

HELENA

Promise.

MONICA

I promise.

HELENA

Tell her…

(Enter GUARDS. HELENA gestures to MONICA.
ASUNCION stands by the door while
JUAN walks over to the bookshelf, takes a
machine gun and starts loading it; he cocks it.
The women look at each other. JUAN
positions himself on the other side of the door.
He receives a call on his walkie-talkie)

JUAN

Sí hermano. Ya vamos.

(GUARDS run out)

HELENA

(Sits down at the table)

Oh my God!!! Hell must be like this.

MONICA

(Places a hand on HELENA'S shoulder)

Take a deep breath.

(Both women breathe)

Let it go.

(Turns around)

How do I look?

HELENA

Like a whore.

MONICA

And you don't? Look at that shirt! It's indecent. You're coming out of it.

HELENA

I think it's sexy. You should see the way COMANDANTE stares at me.

MONICA

What?

Act 2, Scene One

HELENA

(Notices the orchid, picks it up and inhales its aroma)

Hmm. He's so thoughtful.

(Puts orchid in her hair)

He's powerful, a man of the world. Did you know he has a law degree?

MONICA

Yes, but AGUJA is also calculating and cold to run this organization.

HELENA

There's a softer side to him, it's almost as if he wanted to open up, to confide in you, but he can't. Come on, tell me what happened between the two of you.

MONICA

We had some great conversations… then you came along.

HELENA

Face it. Revolutionaries appeal to you.

MONICA

Why do you say that?

HELENA

You had that affair with Ramirez, the epitome of the rebel man, the non-conformist.

MONICA

That's not why I had a relationship with him; you wouldn't understand.

HELENA

Doesn't COMANDANTE AGUJA remind you of your guerrilla fighter?

MONICA

No. My GUERRILLA FIGHTER, as you call him, was more sophisticated. You can keep AGUJA.

HELENA

I'm glad that's settled. I wouldn't want us to fight over him.

(Takes the bag from MONICA)

Let's see what else is in the bag.

(Starts looking through it)

Ha! Lipstick! I wonder where he got it.

MONICA

He keeps it around for his whores.

HELENA

They all fight over him. JUAN told me COMANDANTE has supposedly slept with most of them.

MONICA

(Looks around the room)

I guess there's little else to do around here.

HELENA

(Examines MONICA'S hair)

Let me fix your hair.

(Fixes MONICA'S hair)

So, did you sleep with him?

Act 2, Scene One

MONICA

I'm not telling you.

HELENA

I'll put it in your bio.

MONICA

Will you stop talking about my bio? It makes me feel like
I'm already dead.

(Touches her hair)

I can't believe we got all dressed up.

HELENA

(Puts lipstick on and smacks her lips)

It could save our lives. I heard AGUJA once shot a woman
because he didn't like her lipstick.

MONICA

That's ridiculous! COMANDANTE would never do that.

(A shot is heard)

HELENA

Are you defending him?

MONICA

I can't justify what he does.

HELENA

(HELENA points to the door)

LOOK! THE DOOR! It gives me the creeps just to look
at it.

MONICA

Let's see if it's locked.

(As MONICA and HELENA are about to start walking towards the door COMANDANTE enters. He takes the same glass HELENA has just used and drinks)

COMANDANTE

Ladies, how good of you to come!

MONICA

Did we have a choice?

COMANDANTE

(Ignores her comment; pours them each a glass of aguardiente)

I'm glad you're here for Christmas.

(They toast. To HELENA)

You look ravishing. That blouse suits you well.

(His eyes linger on her décolleté. MONICA looks away)

HELENA

Thanks for the orchid. It's beautiful.

COMANDANTE

Actually…

MONICA

Don't you think it suits her well?

COMANDANTE

(Walks up to MONICA)

You have a stain here.

(Points close to her heart)

Act 2, Scene One

MONICA

It's my broken heart.

COMANDANTE

I told them to wash the clothes, those morons!

HELENA

Where did our clothes come from?

COMANDANTE

Other visitors like you. That one there,

> *(Points at MONICA'S blouse)*

a Danish tourist wore it. She was in her twenties. I'll never forget her look of surprise when she saw the gun.

MONICA

Why did you kill her?

COMANDANTE

Her government refused to pay the ransom. But she had a good time while she was here. She got all the dope she wanted. Half my men enjoyed her.

> *(MONICA paces around the room)*

HELENA

Let's not talk about foreigners, let's dance.

> *(Walks over to the stereo and starts looking through the compact disks. Chooses one by CARLOS VIVES and plays it, continues looking through CDs)*

COMANDANTE

(Moves to the music)

Whom shall I dance with?

(Looks at both women)

HELENA

(To MONICA)

Wait! MONICA, I think I found something you'll like.

(Plays La Traviata, "The Toast" Act One part three. While the music plays HELENA, MONICA and the COMANDANTE toast and drink)

COMANDANTE

Ah, *La Traviata!*

MONICA

(To COMANDANTE)

I didn't know you liked opera.

COMANDANTE

I don't listen to it often. It makes me cry. Please turn it off.

HELENA

(Turns music off)

So are you married COMANDANTE?

COMANDANTE

It's none of your business.

Act 2, Scene One

HELENA

(Looks at his boots)

You polished your boots.

COMANDANTE

(Shows MONICA and HELENA his boots)

I'm fond of these boots; they've saved my life more than once. I don't like to take them off; it's like being without my gun.

HELENA

It IS a different world out here.

COMANDANTE

I prefer it. Survival is about details. Having enough food, enough water, enough ammunition.

(He fumbles with his pockets looking for something)

Some gringos talked to us about a plan to re-introduce guerrilla fighters into society. The World Bank gave them a grant. That's typical of them! They want to help us savages re-enter the civilized world. To them, our country is a back room.

(MONICA and HELENA glance at each other)

HELENA

What do you mean?

COMANDANTE

All houses have a junk room full of boxes you don't want. That's what we are to the gringos, the back room for poverty, drugs, violence. They need us to keep the rest of the house clean.

the Backroom

MONICA

We're not the only ones.

COMANDANTE

Of course not! Theirs is a LARGE back room. The irony is that in the so-called civilized world, one can die for making love; what could be more barbaric than that?

HELENA

Nowadays, that could happen anywhere.

COMANDANTE

(Looks at MONICA and HELENA)

True. But you're probably safer here with me.

(Takes his gun out and cocks it)

Perhaps we should teach the gringos how to leave civilization behind.

(To MONICA)

What are you thinking?

MONICA

That we all have a back room where we keep our darkest secrets, those parts of ourselves we're not proud of.

COMANDANTE

(Continues to look for something around the room)

EXACTLY!

HELENA

I love secrets! That's why I became a journalist.

Act 2, Scene One

COMANDANTE

(Stops in front of MONICA and looks at her for a moment)

(To HELENA)

So you could dig in people's back rooms and come up with their darkest secrets? I've run out of cigars. It's killing me. Fidel sends me a shipment every once in a while. Now, there's a fine man! He doesn't take orders from anyone! I've been told I look like him.

(Stands up straight; MONICA and HELENA glance at each other. COMANDANTE comes close to MONICA and takes her chin)

You look like you've lost weight. That's not good. A skinny woman is not as captivating.

HELENA

That's not what you told me!

COMANDANTE

(Brings his face close to MONICA'S and looks into her eyes, then closes his eyes and inhales)

I like your smell.

MONICA

COMANDANTE, please. I haven't had the luxury of a shower.

COMANDANTE

You can always swim in the river.

MONICA

With the piranhas? No thank you.

COMANDANTE

Ah, you heard about the French attaché. I don't go in the river unless it's on a canoe, but some foreigners have such romantic notions about the Amazon.

HELENA

Wouldn't it be nice to bathe in lavender bubble bath, soft music in the background and candles all around? Just you and your love.

(Looks at COMANDANTE)

COMANDANTE

I'm afraid I can't arrange that. The last time I was in a tub with a woman…

(Looks at MONICA)

But if you have any other requests, I'm feeling generous; it's Christmas.

HELENA

I want Chanel Number Five!

MONICA

I asked for my favorite shower gel but I haven't seen it yet.

COMANDANTE

What's that?

MONICA

Le Must by Cartier. It would camouflage any unpleasant scent.

Act 2, Scene One

COMANDANTE

(Takes a deep breath)

I like your unique aroma; nowadays, people try to hide smells with soaps and gels and perfumes and whatnot. That's the gringo influence, a sign of being civilized. But there's nothing like the natural smell; it draws you in.

(Gets closer to MONICA and inhales again)

Yours is particularly captivating! I could recognize you in a crowd of a thousand women even with a blindfold on.

HELENA

What about me?

COMANDANTE

(Ignores HELENA; to MONICA)

I can't believe you're acting shy with me after everything that's happened.

(He turns to HELENA)

Is this the same woman who was distributing Viagra during her sexually charged campaign?

HELENA

Yes.

COMANDANTE

(To HELENA)

Well, you should know. You're a reporter. Who stopped her? The government or the Catholic Church?

HELENA

I don't remember.

COMANDANTE

(Laughs)

I bet it got the Pope going!

(To HELENA)

You don't remember? What kind of a journalist are you?
And you…

(Turns to MONICA)

You've spent too many years abroad. Do you really think
the men in this country would vote for you? They would
never admit they have a problem that a pill or a woman can
solve. It amazes me that you came back from Italy to save
us!

MONICA

All my life I've traveled, first with my parents and then
with my husband. Rome, London, Paris, Madrid, Istanbul.
I studied English, French, and Italian; became fluent
enough to converse with people in their own language.
In Italy I was Italian; in Spain Spanish; but I was never
myself. No matter where I went I dreamed about our
orchids, smelled their scent in my sleep. I longed for home,
and THIS is home to me. Why wouldn't I come back? Our
country is beautiful. I've never seen such green fields
anywhere else. And the mountains…

HELENA

I thought you dreamt about *almojabanas*.

Act 2, Scene One

COMANDANTE

(To MONICA)

While you were flying around the world in the Concord I was here trying to clean this mess up. Believe me. Sometimes you feel like an immigrant in your own land. And what is worse is that the place you yearn for is an imaginary island far away and out of reach, a place of the heart or the imagination or both that you barely comprehend yourself.

(Pours more drinks, toasts with MONICA while looking straight at her and points to HELENA)

She has better sense than you do. She would've stayed in Europe.

(Strokes HELENA'S cheek. To MONICA)

She's one hundred percent national product.

(Fumbles in his pockets for cigars)

It's a pity one of you...

HELENA

What's for dinner COMANDANTE? I'm starving.

COMANDANTE

We have fresh mango, canned sardines and *aguardiente*.

HELENA

I'm sick of mango.

COMANDANTE

(Takes a mango from the table, and turns it slowly to show how ripe and fresh it is)

The gringos pay five dollars for a mango half as good as this one.

(To MONICA)

Perhaps you would prefer Chianti or Sangiovese with dinner?

MONICA

Aguardiente is fine.

COMANDANTE

Good! I don't approve of spending on foreign products.

(Pours more aguardiente for all of them)

MONICA

If you have spaghetti, I could cook an Italian meal on New Year's Eve.

COMANDANTE

This is a guerrilla camp, not a gourmet restaurant. If you want to cook you'll have to be creative. Great cooks invent meals out of rice and potatoes.

MONICA

Is that all you have?

COMANDANTE

What did you expect? Escargot?

HELENA

MONICA, you told me you didn't know how to cook.

Act 2, Scene One

COMANDANTE

It's still too early to plan for the New Year…

(To himself)

I wish I hadn't told the press.

HELENA

You don't have to do it. You're in charge.

MONICA

If he doesn't keep his word, he'll lose credibility with the new government.

COMANDANTE

I'm glad you understand.

(Sits at the head of the table and motions to MONICA to sit at the place where the orchid was; HELENA sits on the other side. He pours more drinks)

HELENA

COMANDANTE, I noticed you had a tarot deck on the shelf.

COMANDANTE

It belongs to one of my assistants. Do you know how to read it?

HELENA

I learned from my mother. You'd be amazed if I told you who consults with her.

MONICA

Ours has always been a superstitious country.

HELENA

I'm talking about public figures.

COMANDANTE

That's not surprising. No one knows what the hell will happen in this country from one day to the next!

MONICA

(To HELENA)

If your mother's so good, how come she didn't know you would end up here?

HELENA

She warned me not to follow your campaign; *that woman will bring you nothing but trouble,* she said.

MONICA

Well, you should've listened; maybe she'll get you out of here with a little magic.

COMANDANTE

(Snaps his fingers)

The only magic that can liberate you is MY MAGIC. But enough of that; bring the deck. I'll take a card.

(HELENA walks over to the shelf, gets the deck and takes it back to the table. She spreads it. COMANDANTE chooses a card and gives it to her)

Well? What did I get?

HELENA

(Shows the COMANDANTE the card)

The Lovers.

Act 2, Scene One

MONICA

That's a strange card in a place like this.

COMANDANTE

What does it mean?

HELENA

That you'll have to make a choice.

COMANDANTE

I already knew that.

(To MONICA)

Choose one.

(HELENA spreads the cards and MONICA chooses)

HELENA

The eight of swords.

(Shows card to MONICA)

MONICA

Not too promising.

COMANDANTE

Let me see.

(Takes card, studies it)

A woman alone, with a blindfold, tied and surrounded by swords. Is this supposed to be you?

MONICA

I guess. She looks helpless.

HELENA

(Takes card, shows MONICA)

But she's not. Notice the swords; they're not hurting her. The rope around her is loose. She could free herself if she wanted to. This card is about your own perception of captivity versus freedom. What are the ties that bind you? Have you ever thought about it?

COMANDANTE

Let's eat.

*(COMANDANTE, MONICA
and HELENA start eating)*

BLACKOUT

102

While it is still dark a gunshot is heard

Scene Two

Before the lights go up we hear a Gregorian chant and then a prayer, "Hail Mary," recited in Spanish and English by MONICA, HELENA, COMANDANTE and both GUARDS, first separately and then together. The prayer is like a poem, then a song, then a desperate plea.

Hail Mary,
full of grace,
the Lord is with thee.
Blessed art thou amongst women
and blessed is the fruit of thy womb Jesus.
Holy Mary,
Mother of God,
pray for us sinners,
now and at the hour of our death. Amen.

Dios te salve María,
llena eres de gracia,
el Señor es contigo,
bendita eres entre todas las mujeres,
y bendito es el fruto de tu vientre, Jesús.
Santa María,
Madre de Dios,
ruega por nosotros pecadores
ahora y en la hora de nuestra muerte,
amén.

Same room. Dinner leftovers rest on the table. HELENA is throwing up in a bucket in the corner. Enter COMANDANTE; MONICA follows him a few seconds later. She walks over to the table, grabs a napkin and takes it to HELENA.

COMANDANTE

(To HELENA)

Aren't you done?

MONICA

Forgive us. We're not used to witnessing executions.

(HELENA runs out and is heard throwing up off stage. MONICA walks up to COMANDANTE and faces him while he pours more drinks)

What was the purpose of that? I thought I knew you. You're nothing but a cold, calculating murderer.

COMANDANTE

HELENA was curious.

MONICA

She's drunk.

COMANDANTE

She's been asking questions. Plans to write your biography. I think she suspects something. I couldn't leave her out there alone. YOU didn't have to go. I can live with my duality. I'm sorry you can't.

(MONICA picks a glass up and splashes COMANDANTE'S face. He grabs her arms, they look at each other)

Act 2, Scene Two

MONICA

GET YOUR DIRTY HANDS OFF OF ME!

(Enter HELENA with napkin still covering her mouth)

COMANDANTE

(Fills empty glass. Hands HELENA and MONICA glasses)

Drink this. It'll make you feel better.

HELENA

You didn't tell me it would be like that!

COMANDANTE

You journalists are so naïve! Death deserves our attention.
Few are prepared for it.

MONICA

I'll never forget tonight.

COMANDANTE

I made statement to the government and to the world.

(Pours another drink for himself)

Just think.

(Looks at each of them for a while)

It could've been one of you. I bet you were relieved it was
GUTIERREZ instead.

MONICA

You're cruel, COMANDANTE.

COMANDANTE

No, my dear, I'm only human.

MONICA

Why didn't you let me talk to ALICIA?

COMANDANTE

I was protecting you.

MONICA

From what?

HELENA

(Leans on the table)

I don't feel well.

COMANDANTE

You need to step outside to get some fresh air. GUARD!

(Enter ASUNCION)

ASUNCION

Sí, mi COMANDANTE?

COMANDANTE

Not you!

(Exit ASUNCION.
Seconds later JUAN enters)

JUAN

Llamó mi COMANDANTE?

COMANDANTE

Take the lady outside.

(JUAN puts his arm around HELENA
and they exit)

Act 2, Scene Two

MONICA

Do you think she'll be all right?

COMANDANTE

(Places his gun on the table)

She'll be fine. She just needs a little air.

(Places a hand on MONICA'S shoulder)

You're stronger, aren't you?

MONICA

(Puts her hand on his)

Not tonight. I was thinking about the way things were before HELENA came.

COMANDANTE

We had fun.

(Pause)

The other day I remembered the first time we met.

MONICA

Really?

COMANDANTE

Yes. Christmas Eve, at Ramirez's house. I walked in and saw you sitting on the couch. You looked beautiful in your black dress and gold jewelry.

(Turns MONICA around to face him)

The odd thing is you look even better now. The jungle agrees with you.

MONICA

You had a beard. We talked about Europe.

COMANDANTE

That's right! Did you realize while we were talking that we would spend the night together?

MONICA

No. When I asked you to walk me home, I had no idea… I think about that often; wonder why.

COMANDANTE

Why does it rain? Why does the sun shine after a storm? Some things are meant to be.

(Kisses MONICA passionately. She reciprocates)

I miss our time together. I got used to you. I miss your letters.

MONICA

Yours is a strange, irrational love, Armando.

COMANDANTE

No one here knows my name. I like to hear you say it.

MONICA

Armando. Armando.

COMANDANTE

*(Embraces MONICA; looks at her and seems
about to kiss her again)*

What love isn't strange and irrational? Or do you love only with your head?

MONICA

Can a man like you really fall in love that easily? You're the one who stopped sending for me after HELENA came.

COMANDANTE

There's nothing easy about it. How long has it been? Three years? It was becoming dangerous. HELENA is just a distraction. She's attractive and willing. I'm a man.

MONICA

Damn you! How different we are! I've never looked upon intimacy as a distraction.

COMANDANTE

You're not a man.

MONICA

I thought…

COMANDANTE

I'd be with you every night if I could, but I'd be risking your life. If my enemies knew how I feel about you they'd kill you at the first opportunity.

MONICA

Do you have enemies here?

COMANDANTE

Of course I do! What's happened to you? You used to be an expert on intrigue and backstabbing.

MONICA

Is that why you said you plan to execute one of us? To throw your spies off?

COMANDANTE

That's right. Except I've backed myself into a corner. You see, someone took the only picture I had of you from the drawer in my night table. That makes me think they know. I used to look at that picture every night. It reminded me of the way the light fell on your face as you lay next to me.

MONICA

I wish we could spend a whole night together, wake up in each other's arms.

(They embrace)

(Enter ASUNCION; COMANDANTE and MONICA separate)

COMANDANTE

(To ASUNCION)

ASUNCION! One day I'll shoot.

ASUNCION

Sorry, COMANDANTE.

(Glances at MONICA with hatred)

MONICA

(To COMANDANTE)

Thanks for the book.

COMANDANTE

I read it a couple of months ago. We should learn from Tibet. They've been through a lot. If I didn't love this country, I'd move far away. You see, you're not the only who cares about this place.

Act 2, Scene Two

ASUNCION

Excuse me, COMANDANTE. Will you be needing
anything else?

COMANDANTE

No. How's MAYO?

ASUNCION

We took her for a walk. She's better now.

COMANDANTE

Keep an eye on her.

ASUNCION

Sí señor.

(Exit ASUNCION)

111

MONICA

Are you a Buddhist?

COMANDANTE

I believe in reincarnation. Does that make me one?

MONICA

Buddhists don't murder. Aren't you worried about your next
reincarnation?

COMANDANTE

(Embraces MONICA)

No. I've accumulated good karma throughout the centuries.
Besides, the Dalai Lama understands better than anyone
how important it is to fight for FREEDOM.

Buddhism
Dalai Lama

MONICA

In a peaceful manner. He would never approve of violence.

COMANDANTE

So? I guess I'm a black sheep of a Buddhist! We can't all be perfect.

(Kisses MONICA'S head)

I also believe in soul mates. Do you?

MONICA

I'm still waiting for mine to show up.

(COMANDANTE turns on the stereo and plays a bolero)

COMANDANTE

That's not what you said the first night. Let's dance.

(COMANDANTE turns the music up.
MONICA joins him. They dance. HELENA enters,
walks over to the stereo and turns the music off.
MONICA walks away and sits at the table;
COMANDANTE pours more drinks)

HELENA

(To COMANDANTE)

I thought that was OUR song.

(To MONICA)

You're flirting with MY COMANDANTE! Do you think he's yours?

MONICA

Don't be silly.

(To COMANDANTE)

She's drunk.

HELENA

I'M NOT DRUNK!

COMANDANTE

(To MONICA)

Would it be such a ridiculous idea?

MONICA

We're too different.

(Picks her glass up and studies it)

This stuff is strong. I don't think I should have anymore.

COMANDANTE

(Pours more aguardiente in MONICA'S glass)

Do you remember what you wrote? I do.

(Hands MONICA her glass and raises his own to toast)

Please drink. What do you have to lose? We could all be dead tomorrow.

(Drinks)

How do you say please in Italian?

MONICA

Prego.

> *(Drinks; HELENA drinks too)*

HELENA, a minute ago you were throwing up. Stop.

HELENA

> *(Gulps her drink, slams the glass on the table and grabs COMANDANTE'S gun. She points it at MONICA)*

Are YOU going to tell ME what to do? Only my COMANDANTE can order me around! I'LL SHOOT YOU!!

COMANDANTE

HELENA!!! It's a miracle you haven't gotten yourself killed. Put that gun down. Now! IT'S AN ORDER!

114

HELENA

Not yet, *mi amor.* I have to get rid of her first.

COMANDANTE

Don't do it. Be a good girl.

> *(Walks closer to HELENA and tries to take the gun from her)*

HELENA

I'M TIRED OF BEING A GOOD GIRL. YOU LOOK AT HER IN A WAY YOU'VE NEVER LOOKED AT ME! I WON'T LET IT HAPPEN. I WANT TO LIVE! I CHOOSE TO LIVE!

> *(To COMANDANTE)*

I WON'T KILL HER IF YOU DO IT.

Act 2, Scene Two

(HELENA shoots but misses. GUARDS rush in;
COMANDANTE takes the gun from HELENA.
MONICA rests her head on the table)

COMANDANTE

(To GUARDS, pointing at HELENA)

GET HER OUT OF HERE!

ASUNCION

Sí, mi COMANDANTE.

(Walks up to MONICA)

Too bad she missed!

JUAN

(To HELENA)

Come on, *Corazón*, I'll take you for another nice walk.

*(Puts his arm around HELENA and tries to lead her out of
the room but she fights back; the GUARDS drag her out)*

HELENA

NO! NO! LET GO OF ME, YOU IDIOTS!!

*(As the GUARDS are dragging HELENA out,
she stops in front of MONICA)*

HELENA

I'M NOT DONE WITH YOU YET!!!!

(GUARDS and HELENA exit)

BLACKOUT

the Backroom

116

Scene Three

Same room. COMANDANTE and MONICA sit at the table.

COMANDANTE

I think she's fallen for me.

(MONICA looks up at him)

MONICA

WHAT A GREAT SATISFACTION THAT MUST BE!

COMANDANTE

I thought my interest in her would distract attention away from you. I even told the GUARDS you had rejected me.

MONICA

How do you REALLY feel about HELENA?

COMANDANTE

She's a sweet girl.

MONICA

I'm not sure that's how I would describe her.

COMANDANTE

You can't blame her for her ambition and her desire to succeed. Perhaps you were once like that yourself.

(Pours another drink)

Here, take a sip, *prego.*

(MONICA takes a sip from his glass while he holds it; they look at each other for a minute)

You remind me of *Tosca.*

MONICA

That would make you Caravadossi.

COMANDANTE

Let's hope we fare better than they did.

MONICA

Oh, but their love! *L'amore!*

COMANDANTE

When I was young, I wanted to learn Italian.

MONICA

I'll teach you.

COMANDANTE

And what good will Italian do me? In this country we don't understand each other and we all speak the same language.

MONICA

I know, but…

118

Act 2, Scene Three

COMANDANTE

(Starts pacing around the room)

BUT WHAT? WHAT DO YOU KNOW ABOUT THIS COUNTRY? WHAT DO YOU KNOW ABOUT OUR NEEDS? WHAT DO YOU KNOW ABOUT HUNGER AND POVERTY?

(Stands in front of MONICA and faces her)

I grew up, like you, in the lap of luxury. Drivers, servants, private clubs, trips to Miami and to Europe.

(Starts pacing again, stops in front of MONICA)

But what I saw while I was driven around the city streets was poverty, children under bridges, the cardboard boxes they lived in. One night I met Father Perez. He died in my arms.

MONICA

I understand.

COMANDANTE

HOW CAN YOU UNDERSTAND? You grew up in a mansion in Rome; I heard Neruda and Márquez were frequent visitors in your home.

(Looks at MONICA. Her eyes are closed and she's nodding. He takes his gun and holds it to her head)

LISTEN TO ME!

(MONICA sits up straight and opens her eyes)

I HATE PEOPLE LIKE YOU! Privileged people that think the world owes them something. Sophisticated people. What a waste!

MONICA

Please put that gun away.

COMANDANTE

(Pushes the gun harder against her head)

I'll put it away when I please. You're not listening to me.
What are you thinking?

MONICA

I was thinking about my children.

COMANDANTE

Feeling guilty? Don't you think it's a little late for that?
After all, you abandoned them.

MONICA

I DIDN'T ABANDON THEM! I did what I thought was
right.

COMANDANTE

You shipped them off to their father in New Zealand.
I read your book. Or should I call it manifesto, propaganda?
Once you decided to save this poor country you didn't
hesitate to get rid of your excess baggage.

MONICA

Are you trying to provoke me? Do you expect me to do
something stupid so you can shoot me?

*(Stands up, is about to slap him, hesitates for a moment, and
then kisses him passionately; he reciprocates)*

You want me to hate you but I can't.

Act 2, Scene Three

COMANDANTE

I wish I didn't love you. I wish I hated you. But since that first night, I wondered what it would be like to live with you, to have you in my bed every night, to reach over and stroke your cheek at dawn. I read your letters over and over and even though I never wrote to you . . .

(Paces around the table and then stops in front of MONICA and picks up his gun)

I'm the one who has the gun. Hate comes more naturally to me.

(Points gun at her)

I was getting used to the idea of living without you.

MONICA

Ah, yes. If we could only learn non-attachment from our Buddhist friends. Yet the people you love take over your mind when you're a captive. It's not being a prisoner that bothers me or the treatment that I sometimes get from you; it's what you've done here...

(Points at her heart)

and here.

(Points to her head)

prisoner by what you think + you feel

COMANDANTE

(Walks over to the bookshelf and grabs a piece of paper)

People are writing poems about you. Listen to this…

(He reads)

Monica Delgado/A woman/who dreamt she could be president/ and heal the wounds of all her people/was taken prisoner by fierce GUERRILLA fighters/while out on her campaign.

(Looks at MONICA)

I never thought of myself as "fierce." Did you really hope to cure <u>all your people</u> by becoming president?

MONICA

Do you find it hard to believe that someone would give everything up for their country? Is it because I'm a woman? Men would never have to explain that.

COMANDANTE

Why don't you take care of your own wounds first?

MONICA

What are you talking about?

COMANDANTE

Have you ever heard of Chiron, king of the centaurs? He was wounded by a poisoned arrow, could not heal himself and was condemned to live in pain forever.

MONICA

It's always easier to nurse the wounds of others than your own.

Act 2, Scene Three

COMANDANTE

What drove you back to this country in the first place? Why did you choose to be with me that night? Do you know?

MONICA

I came here because I thought I'd never be kidnapped! It was the beginning of a dialogue without weapons.

(Comandante is about to speak)

If you think I was looking for you… You've been with enough women, Armando, to know that what we had was not ordinary.

COMANDANTE

We briefly touched each others' lives. The army could come and blow us up at any moment. A hundred years from now, you and I will be forgotten and the fact that we walked on this earth, that we kissed and held each other, how much is that going to matter? Freedom will matter; independence will matter, but love?

MONICA

I think only that will matter.

*(Takes poem from COMANDANTE
and studies it)*

But you will always put it last. The revolution comes first.

COMANDANTE

This is my life. They don't pay well, but you find ways to make a little extra. It's amazing how much money people are willing to pay for a little coca.

MONICA

Some take drugs and some get religious.

COMANDANTE

It's unhealthy to become dependent on drugs; religion can
be good for you.

MONICA

Unless you overdose on it. Anything that prevents you from
seeing things as they are is dangerous.

COMANDANTE

(Pours more drinks)

Sometimes things as they REALLY are leave a lot to
be desired. The revolution is not pleasant, but it has to be
completed.

MONICA

Don't you think it's time to end it? Your rebels have become
fanatics; too many people have already died.

COMANDANTE

(Polishing his gun)

You're right. But the revolution is not only our religion,
it's our business. We work with the mafia and the army.
Years ago, when drug traffickers hired us to protect
plantations and labs, we needed the money. Then we
became entrepreneurs.

MONICA

Doesn't selling drugs to young innocent people bother you?

Act 2, Scene Three

COMANDANTE

The gringos are our best customers. I see it as our contribution to the decline of the American Empire. Call it war tactics.

(Points at his gun)

We need to pay for these.

> *(Walks over to the stereo cabinet and pulls out a
> machine gun from the bottom shelf; he carries it
> over to the table and shows it to MONICA)*

This is an AK 47. Pick it up.

> *(MONICA lifts it. COMANDANTE stands behind her and
> embraces her as he shows her how to hold the machine gun;
> his lips brush her neck; MONICA turns and they look
> at each other; neither of them moves or speaks for a moment)*

How does it feel?

MONICA

It's surprisingly light. A child could hold it.

COMANDANTE

Children do. There's something very sensual about it. My men refer to it as their girlfriend.

MONICA

Why not their wife?

COMANDANTE

> *(Takes machine gun from MONICA and
> begins to stroke it gently)*

A wife is loyal, hard working and supportive. A girlfriend can be fickle. Yet she can also give you immense pleasure, pleasure beyond anything you ever imagined.

MONICA

Do all your men have one?

COMANDANTE

Yes. And our women. It's the most reproduced mechanical device in the world. The Russians and the Chinese have given us plenty. The Americans furnish M16s to our army; we benefit from that.

(Moves closer to MONICA and strokes her hair)

I bet my kiss surprised you.

MONICA

Every night I wonder why you stopped sending for me, why you chose to sever all contact. Was it something I said? Something I did? Was I too candid? Did you decide one day, after kissing me and holding me in your arms that you didn't want to bother with me anymore?

(Goes back to examining the machine gun)

COMANDANTE

(Embraces MONICA)

I dreamed about us together. Then I wondered how we would explain it to our families. What would you tell your friends, your children? People would get hurt, and there's enough pain in this world already. Our love is as much of a fantasy as saying that one day we'll have peace.

MONICA

I may not get out of here alive . . .

COMANDANTE

Do you REALLY think I could bear the thought of losing you? Sometimes I dream about seeking asylum in the US.

Act 2, Scene Three

MONICA

That's the right country for a GUERRILLA leader and a former presidential candidate pursuing the American dream!

COMANDANTE

Why not? It's a place where foreigners succeed.

MONICA

I've seen engineers scrubbing toilets and architects driving taxicabs. It all depends on what part of the world you come from.

COMANDANTE

Of course! But we're ALL running away from something; poverty, politics, love.

(Caresses MONICA'S cheek)

MONICA

Ah, the double life of the émigré.

COMANDANTE

Not all immigrants get to stay in five-star hotels.

MONICA

Silk sheets and bubble bath won't erase desolation.

COMANDANTE

No. But they can make it nicer. I must confess I wouldn't mind a night at the Ritz with you.

MONICA

I wonder if, after all these years in the jungle, you could live…

COMANDANTE

In the civilized world? The skills I've learnt here should serve me well. I have a warehouse full of dope. The boys from the CIA offered to buy it; they're willing to pay top dollar for it.

MONICA

Why?

COMANDANTE

To stage the largest bust of the century.

(Takes hold of MONICA'S hands)

We could build a house in Miami, plant a garden, make friends with the disillusioned Cubans, drink *mojitos* while we watch the struggle of our people on *Univision*.

MONICA

Nothing like television to make you feel detached.

COMANDANTE

I'll write a memoir confessing all my sins. That's the American way, right?

(Starts pacing around the room, arms behind his back)

MONICA

I'm not sure you would like the US. Have you ever been there?

COMANDANTE

Once, for business.

MONICA

What kind of business?

Act 2, Scene Three

COMANDANTE

I was part of a delegation attending a peace conference at Harvard ten years ago during the negotiations with the government.

(MONICA sits down)

MONICA

Do you think we'll ever have peace?

COMANDANTE

I don't see it coming. The National Liberation army is just as serious as we are. Our paramilitary forces make US look compassionate!

MONICA

What did you expect? When you started taking over their land, cattle farmers had to fight back.

COMANDANTE

I'm sure they didn't know their army would slaughter whole villages. It's very sad.

(Puts machine gun back on the shelf)

MONICA

Did you like the US?

COMANDANTE

I was appalled by the marketing spirit that drives the whole country. I got some insights about Americans, though.

MONICA

Such as?

COMANDANTE

They still believe in fairy tales and in the good guy/bad guy formula like their children. Gringos don't understand that human nature is much, much more complex than that.

(Faces MONICA)

Look at you, for instance. On the one hand, you're bright, ambitious and attractive.

(Passes his finger around her lips)

On the other hand, you're capable of becoming a whore and selling yourself to the Europeans. Do you realize how humiliating that is for us? Do you think we enjoy watching you air our dirty laundry in your manifesto? We've already suffered enough, first in the hands of the Spaniards and now with the gringos.

MONICA

(Slaps him)

I AM NO ONE'S WHORE!

*(COMANDANTE seems about to retaliate.
In a conciliatory tone)*

I'm sorry you didn't like my book.

COMANDANTE

YOU DON'T CARE ABOUT MY OPINION! All you care about is your best seller, translated into twenty languages. Europeans and Americans love you; you're their heroine. But I know you didn't write all the truth in your book.

MONICA

What do you mean?

Act 2, Scene Three

COMANDANTE

You didn't mention your affair with Ramirez, my colleague turned senator.

MONICA

That's my private life.

COMANDANTE

HOW CONVENIENT! I thought the whole book was about your private life and your struggles to save your people. I must give you credit. You convinced half the world. Actually, by getting yourself kidnapped you have managed to become a celebrity, even if you never had a shot at the presidency.

(Moves closer to MONICA as if to kiss her)

Wasn't Ramirez imprisoned for corruption?

MONICA

He was unfairly accused.

COMANDANTE

Well, life isn't fair now, is it? If it were, I wouldn't be threatening you and you wouldn't be begging me to let you go.

MONICA

I HAVEN'T BEGGED YOU TO LET ME GO!

COMANDANTE

Sometimes I see your hatred, your eagerness to be rid of me. If I were not the torturer and you were not the victim, we might have a chance.

(Kisses her. She reciprocates)

Why are you here?

MONICA

EXCUSE ME? You kidnapped me.

COMANDANTE

<u>No. You came to us</u>. We just kept you. But I'm talking about something else. Why did you come here in the first place? Why did you leave Italy, your husband, a comfortable life, your children? Have you ever asked yourself that question?

MONICA

Unfinished business. Karma.

COMANDANTE

Let's finish it now. We have time. Why such a need to change, to leave everything behind?

MONICA

(Pensive. Walks around the room)

I wanted to help my country.

COMANDANTE

You wanted to help yourself! There's a lot of people out there that want to help this country. But they don't do what you did. I think your political career and your campaign for the presidency were about something else. You're running away from something.

MONICA

From what?

COMANDANTE

You tell me.

Act 2, Scene Three

MONICA

(Sits down, takes her glass and drinks)

Armando, most of my life I've compromised.

COMANDANTE

You would make a good politician then.

MONICA

Not anymore, I'm afraid. I tried to be a good daughter, mother and wife, but with time my husband and I grew apart; then I discovered the truth about my parents' marriage; they've never loved each other. Father has a mistress and I can't say I blame him. So I turned to my career and discovered that I hate politics and everything politicians represent: hypocrisy, double dealing, chauvinism and corruption. After living in Europe for so long, the chaos in this place appealed to me. Sure, it's gotten out of hand, but it was refreshing to meet people that believed in change and in ME. I wonder; what gives life meaning? Is it detail? The daily routine that we engage in? Or is it change, being shaken to your roots and coming out a different person?

COMANDANTE

So you are as much of a rebel as I am! I freed you from your obligations. Now no one expects you to be a candidate for the green party or to clean up the mess that others made of things. You don't have to be a dutiful daughter, wife or mother, do you? Perhaps you'll never go back to that. The world is full of people stranded in meaningless jobs or dead relationships. If they could, they would start over again. I've given you the opportunity.

(Sits down, starts unlacing his boots)

Do you mind if I take these off?

MONICA

No. I didn't know I would end up here with you, Armando, and what's more, I didn't think I would want to stay. One day I woke up and thought, half of my life is over, and what have I done? Whatever happened to those ideals I had as a young student in Rome, when my friends and I spent hours sitting at outdoor cafes in Piazza Navonna discussing politics and world hunger? When we staged demonstrations against the government and looked up to the members of the Red Brigades? Here I was, living in a mansion, with a chauffeur, atending cocktail parties with my husband, shopping on Via Veneto and Piazza Spagna. The worst part of it was that I enjoyed it. I'm here because of you and to show my children that they should listen to their hearts. I guess that would make me a romantic. Yes, MONICA DELGADO, presidential candidate for the green party, privileged jet setter and mother of two, is an idealist, a romantic and a fearlessly ambitious woman. So shoot me.

COMANDANTE

(Smiles)

In another century, you would've been burned at the stake.

MONICA

Who says I'm not going to pay a price now?

COMANDANTE

Me. The inquisitor has lost his heart.

(Takes his boots off)

What was it like with the Italian?

(MONICA remains silent)

COMANDANTE

You don't have the right to remain silent!! THIS IS NOT A DEMOCRACY!

MONICA

What is it like with your wife?

COMANDANTE

<u>What is it like with my wife?</u> It's like having a double life. She doesn't understand my world any more than I do hers. You know, marriage is passion's worst enemy.

MONICA

Without marriage, society would collapse.

COMANDANTE

OH, REALLY? Is that why you divorced your husband and took up with RAMIREZ?

MONICA

I divorced my husband because I could no longer live his life.

COMANDANTE

You went out and found yourself a great life, didn't you? How ironic! MASSIMILIANO CONTI may be the one who saves you.

MONICA

What do you mean?

COMANDANTE

He pressured the Italian government to ask for your release and now the Italians are convincing the Americans to help negotiate with our forces.

MONICA

(Looks at him)

What release?

COMANDANTE

Haven't you heard? The new president has softened his position. That shouldn't surprise you. I knew it would happen sooner or later. His tough approach was never going to work. We're not children. We don't need to be disciplined, to learn a lesson. The gringos like to teach their enemies lessons. How dangerous.

MONICA

What about my release?

COMANDANTE

So you can go back and be a heroine all over again? Don't get your hopes up. It's not a done deal. I'm talking to the boys from the CIA. If you do get out, you should thank CONTI.

MONICA

MASSIMILIANO is a politician. My release would be a feather in his cap.

(Takes another sip from her glass)

Figures he would go out and try to save me; do what's best for me. The problem is, he's never known what IS best for me. MASSIMILIANO has never listened to anyone but himself.

(To COMANDANTE)

My release would increase your power.

Act 2, Scene Three

COMANDANTE

Don't talk to me about power, you who have so much power over me!

MONICA

What good is it if I can't have your love? Think about your image.

COMANDANTE

WHAT THE HELL DO I CARE ABOUT MY IMAGE? Do you think I care if your life and your struggles are posted all over the Internet? If more than a hundred countries made you an honorary citizen? The mayor of Rome extended an invitation for you to vacation there after your liberation. People are writing poetry about you. DO YOU THINK I CARE? I DON'T GIVE A SHIT.

(Rests his hands on her shoulders)

Because, you see, my dear, your life is in my hands.

(Takes the gun)

I could pull this trigger and annihilate you in one second and there are no governments that could save you if I decide you should not live.

MONICA

Then why don't you shoot me now and put me out of my misery?

COMANDANTE

I don't feel like it. I can't.

(Seems about to kiss her)

Come. There's something I want to show you. Take your shoes off.

the Backroom

(MONICA takes her shoes off and follows COMANDANTE to the back of the room where the door remains closed. ASUNCION enters from the opposite side of the stage. Neither MONICA nor COMANDANTE notice her)

BLACKOUT

Scene Four

*MONICA and COMANDANTE stand in front of the red
door while ASUNCION watches from a distance.*

COMANDANTE

See this door? It's always locked. No one is allowed to open
it but me. Tonight you'll discover what's in there.

(Sees ASUNCION)

But first you have to guess. If you guess right you live; if
you guess wrong you die. Go to sleep now. I'll call for you
later. You have the rest of the night to think about it.

*(Tries to let MONICA know about
ASUNCION but she doesn't understand.
ASUNCION observes MONICA with contempt)*

MONICA

If you don't mind, I'd rather get it over with.

COMANDANTE

Always up for an adventure! Okay. You get three guesses.
I'll blindfold you so you can concentrate.

*(Pulls a scarf out of his pocket and blindfolds MONICA.
When he's done, he kisses her neck while ASUNCION watches)*

I'll open the door so you can engage all your senses.

the Backroom

(Takes a key out of his shirt pocket and proceeds to open the door. Lights go on behind the scrim to reveal thousands of lit candles in the background. Statuettes of saints become visible behind the scrim. To the corner is one of the Virgin Mary)

MONICA

It's hot in there. You have a fire.

COMANDANTE

Close.

MONICA

It's not a torture room.

(Inhales slowly)

There's a profound silence and a smell of, what, what is it? Ah, yes! Wax. Candles! You have candles! It's a chapel.

COMANDANTE

(Takes MONICA'S blindfold off and points the gun at her head)

Good guess. You owe your life to the Virgin. *La Virgencita* saved you.

MONICA

(Falls to her knees)

Oh my God!

Act 2, Scene Four

COMANDANTE

(Places his hand on MONICA'S shoulder)

This is my world, my refuge, the place where I find peace, pray, meditate. In front of all these saints my hands are free of blood stains. My heart is pure and filled with love for all humanity. The saints have taught me to be humble, to be patient and to suffer, as they have, for this imperfect world.

(Bows his head in prayer. To MONICA)

Pray to the Virgin. She'll listen to you. Every morning I come in here and light a candle in her honor. Every time I must kill someone I pray for their soul. I pray for our country. I pray for peace. I pray for us, and now I pray for you.

(ASUNCION stares at the BACK ROOM.
Enter JUAN.
He walks over to the room in awe)

COMANDANTE

What do you want *huevón*? Can't you see I'm busy?

JUAN

Sorry, mi COMANDANTE. Mr. Michaels is here.

COMANDANTE

Who?

JUAN

Mr. Michaels, the gringo from the CIA; he's here to take her back.

(Points to MONICA)

COMANDANTE

(Gives MONICA a hand to help her stand;
<u>*MONICA looks at him and shakes her head no.*</u>
COMANDANTE turns to JUAN)

Tell him he can have the reporter instead. I'm not ready to give our heroine up yet.

(MONICA and COMANDANTE
look at each other, her hand still in his)

(In the dark, the "Memorare" is recited in Spanish
and English by MONICA and COMANDANTE AGUJA.
As in the First Act, it begins as a poem and ends as a
desperate plea. A Gregorian chant plays)

Memorare
by
Fray Luis de Granada
1588

No me desampare tu amparo,

no me falte tu piedad,

no me olvide tu memoria.

Si tú, Señora, me dejas, ¿quién me sostendra?

Si tú me olvidas, ¿quién se acordará de mí?

Si tú, que eres Estrella de la mar

y guía de los errados, no me alumbras,

¿dónde iré a parar?

No me dejes tentar del enemigo,

y si me tentare, no me dejes caer,

y si cayere, ayúdame a levantar.

¿Quién te llamó, Señora, que no le oyeses?

¿Quién te pidió, que no le otorgases?

Act 2, Scene Four

Memorare

by

Fray Luis de Granada

May your protection always shelter me
may I have your compassion
may you keep me in your memory.
For if you forsake me who will support me?
If you forget me who will remember me?
If you, the star of the seas
and guide of the lost, don't enlighten me,
what will become of me?
Don't let the enemy tempt me.
and if he were to tempt me, don't let me fall,
and if I were to fall, help me rise.
For who ever called you, lady, without being heard?
Who asked and did not receive?

BLACKOUT

THE END